Nihil Obstat, Arthur J. Scanlan, S.T.D., Censor Liborum
Imprimatur ✠ Francis Cardinal Spellman,
Archbishop of New York
Cum Permissu Superiorum

William J. Hirten Co., Cumberland, RI

G L O R I A
Children's Books

The Boy Jesus

"The Perfect Child"

by Daniel A. Lord, S.J.

Sometimes your father tells you,
"That's a fine boy."
That makes you feel very happy.
Sometime your mother tells you,
"That's my good girl."
And that makes you smile.
But sometimes your dad says, "Why must you be bad?" and mother says, "You really have been very naughty today." Then we are sorry and ashamed. When is a boy or a girl really good? When are they really bad and naughty? Maybe you find it hard to be sure.
You wish someone would make goodness and badness very clear. Someone did. That was the dear Lord Jesus.

God our Father made this beautiful world.
Then He made all the men and
women, the boys and girls, in it.
"These are My sons and daughters," He
said, "I want them to be very happy."
So He gave them everything
to make them happy.
But they weren't always.
Sometimes they stole from one another.
Sometimes they were wicked and they
fought. Sometimes they even killed.
They were unkind.
They were often very cruel.
God said, "Please be good.
If you are, you will be happy."
Many of them said, "We don't want to be
good. We want to be bad."
So they were very unhappy.

7

At last God our Father said, "I will ask
My Son, Jesus Christ to show them
how to be good and happy."
So Jesus Christ was born on the first
Christmas Day.
Jesus made Mary
and Joseph very happy.
Mary was His dear Mother,
Joseph was His foster father.
As a little baby,
He loved them very much.
He laughed and stretched out
His arms to them.

But when He became a little boy,
He proved He really loved them.
He never did anything
mean or disobedient.
He helped His Mother in her kitchen.
He ran errands for Joseph.
When they asked Him to do
anything, He did it right away.
Mary and Joseph never had to worry
about Him. They never wondered
where He was. They never said,
"I hope He is not up to any mischief."
For He was a good and obedient Son.
He made them wonderfully happy.
He made their home the happiest
place in the world.

When Jesus was twelve years old,
Joseph and Mary took Him to
Jerusalem where the Temple stood.
The Jewish Temple
was God's house on earth.
Jesus loved His Father's house.
So when Mary and Joseph
returned to Nazareth, their home,
He stayed behind.
He knew that God wished Him to
stay longer in His Father's House.
Soon Mary and Joseph
found that Jesus was lost.
They hurried back to the Temple.
For three days and nights
the looked everywhere for Him.

Finally, they found Him seated
among the doctors and priests.
He was asking them wise questions
and teaching them about the Savior.
He did this because this was
"His Father's business."
Then quietly He returned to Nazareth
with Joseph and Mary
and for the rest of His youth,
He was perfectly obedient to them.
All His life Jesus loved His friends.
Later on, He did wonderful things
called miracles to make them happy.
He cured the sick.
He even raised the dead.
He told them wonderful things
about the next world.

As a boy, Jesus loved His friends.
He played ball with them.
He played games with them.
He walked in the woods with them.
Never did He fight or act mean.
He was friendly to strange boys and
girls who came to live near Him.
He let the other boys and girls play
with the toys that Joseph
made for Him.
He was much smarter than them.
But He never showed off.
He never looked down on them.
So all the boys and girls loved
to play with Jesus.
"He is the finest friend in the world,"
they said.

Mary, His dear Mother, taught Him
to read and write.
Later, when He was older, He went to the
little village school. It was near the
synagogue, which was the name
for the church.
He wanted to learn.
He learned to read so that He could
read the Bible.
He studied arithmetic so that He could
help Joseph with his work.

Jesus loved to pray.
He knew when He prayed,
He talked to His Father in heaven.
But never did He sin.
Sin makes people so unhappy.
"Whatever you want Me to do, Father,"
He said, "I will do."

He read books of history.
Some day, He knew He was going to be
the great Physician. And doctors have
to be smart.
He was also going to be a great Judge.
And judges must be wise.
He was going to be the greatest Teacher.
And teachers have to know a great deal.
So He studied very hard. He never
neglected His lessons. He never said,
"I hate to study."
And He grew up very bright and He knew
a great many important things.
Naturally He became a very wise man.

Sin is the thing that makes us most unhappy.
Yes, sin is the thing that makes
the world so sad.
Bad boys make their Mothers and Fathers
very unhappy.
Bad girls make their parents weep.
But Jesus never committed a sin. He never hit
anyone. He never even wanted things that
belonged to someone else. He always told the
truth. He was kind and generous.
So He made everyone happy.
Other boys trusted Him.
They liked to play with Him.
Little girls knew He would never hurt them.
He was not rough or unkind.
So even when He was little,
He made everyone happy.

Why does Dad want you to be a good boy?
Because if you are, you will grow up
to be a fine man.
Why does Mother want you to be a good girl?
Because if you are, you will become
a lovely woman.
Bad boys become bad men.
Bad girls become mean women.
And bad men and mean women make the
world very unhappy.
Jesus knew this. So He was the best boy
that ever lived.
He loved God, His Father. He was
obedient to Mary, His Mother, and Joseph,
His foster father. He studied hard. He said
His prayers. He was kind to other boys and
girls. He never sinned.

When He grew up, Jesus Christ was the
greatest Man that ever lived.
But first, He was the best Child
that ever lived.
God was His Father. He knew that God
made the food that He ate. He made the
beautiful sky overhead. He made wool and
cotton for His clothes.
He put love in the hearts of
Mary and Joseph.
So Jesus loved His heavenly Father.
"I want to do good always," He said. "I
want to make everyone happy. That was
Our Father's plan for His children.

No wonder He grew up to be the greatest
Man that ever lived.
Don't you want to grow up to be
like Him?
Don't you want to make the
world happier?
Then be a good friend like Jesus.
Try to be as fine a child as Jesus was.
If you are like the Boy Jesus, you will grow
up to be a person everyone loves.
You will make the world around you
very beautiful.